Aakashvaani

Whenever the Oracles in the Welkin thunder, Resonance finds Home in our Hearts and Minds.

Aarav Sureka

Made with ❤ on the BookLeaf Publishing Platform
www.bookleafpub.in
www.bookleafpub.com

Dedication

This book is undoubtedly for my parents, who are the two people from whom I draw support each day; two people who have never told anyone those secret facts about me which might assure them that I am a crazy maniac; two people without the assistance of whom this book would have had no title.

Preface

'Aakashvaani' is a collection of 21 poems which are aimed at taking readers on a voyage in the ship of words tossed upon the seas of time. Through this anthology, I hope to accompany readers on an odyssey through human emotions, and the internal and external storms in man's mind that develop underneath the expansive shade of the thundering firmament. It is a journey through feelings and sentiments, through patriotism, true love and affection, tragedies, comedies, satire, social criticism, and motivation, and through rejuvenation and celebration. The welkin is studded with twinkling stars and it stretches above us and further beyond, serving as a gateway both to the Heavens and the black void of the unseen and the unknown. And everything that happens on this earth happens below this sky:

Whenever the oracles from this sky blaze forth their stories through the thunder and the lightning, if we close our eyes and try to listen to the music to which the cosmos dances, we will hear the eternal voice of the Heavens: a very clear voice from the skies. When we strive to walk forward on this never-ending journey of life, we will reach closer to our destination - we will be able to develop the frequency which matches with the Divine song, there will be resonance and then, we will be

able to hear, loud and clear, the voice of the sky -
"Aakashvaani".

Acknowledgements

I would definitely be always indebted towards my parents, who have always been my constant supporters and have assisted me in each phase of the drafting of this book. I would also like to thank all my teachers, who have made me capable of writing this book. I would especially be grateful to two of them all - the one who has impacted my poetry a lot, and the one who has made it possible for the transformation of a manuscript into a book. I would express my gratitude towards my near and dear ones, my relatives and friends and all-time readers, who always complimented my poetry and inspired me to write more. I would thank Mr. William Shakespeare, Kobiguru Rabindranath Tagore, and Mr. Robert Frost, who have hopefully allowed me to allude to a few of their epic works and quotes somewhere in some piece. I would also be obliged to Shri Krishna, for the blessings of the Almighty have helped me throughout this journey. Lastly, I would be grateful to BookLeaf Publishing, which provided me a platform to realise a dream.

I. Free Fire

The sparks of the Flame
Embracing the darkness of the sky.
Shall the World remember his name?
The selfish World has no time to cry.

O, ye Fire! Let thyself break free -
Engulf the lost warrior
Who is yet to see
How his sacrifice
Shall bring us victory!

'tis the World that creates this mutual strife;
'tis the World that doth take 'way his life.
And now, 'tis the same World
That shall forget the unsung soldier
Whose Valour when unfurl'd
Would terribly shake the coward enemy:
'tis the same World
That shall forget him - what a pity!

Yet we shall remember him, always -
O, ye bold son of our Land!
O, ye brave hart, worthy of praise,
Why did thee fall at the hunters' hand?

Worry not, O Comrade -
Thou hast never known fear:
Let thyself know, that thy hunters' end is near -
O, my Friend, can thou hear?
Your effort shall ne'er go in vain,
For those Demons shall truly understand what is pain:

For no Sword will bow to sea or land,
In front on the immortal job at hand:
'tis the heart that throbs for the motherland,
'tis the heart that leads us thro' the sand,
'tis the heart that makes us take a stand.

O, ye Fire! Let thyself break free -
Spread and spread, far and wide;
Let the dogs of war roam free to see
That we shall find them, O Comrades,
No matter where they hide.

And, O Comrades, we shall ne'er forget,
Upon what mission, our foot is set:
And for our Nation, an' for our friend,
We still have a lot to lend -

For a true soldier never wants to know
What his country did for him,
But what he did for his motherland

Risking himself to the brim:

For the self is nothing.
We are nothing but mortal men,
Wayfarers on this blissful path of life
That He has gifted us with. And then
Knowing that this path
Has one necessary end,
We shall ne'er hesitate,
When Duty calls on us to lend
Our life for the nation, just like our friend.

O Warriors, here we proceed
Into the battlefield
Where the Fire has broken free.
Let's bid goodbye
For we do not know
What Fate wants us to see.

O Comrades, be quick,
Fight with brain and brawn.
A shot and a spark -
O, my Friends! Another companion is gone.

His blood thus flows out silently.
Yet, we shall not cry -
Remember friends, now none of you

Has got any time to die -

Now Duty calls upon me,
Let not its call be delay'd -
I am going, my Friends,
But promise to me,
That none of you shall be dismay'd.

Before you see the Tricolour
Hoisted proudly 'bove your head,
Promise to me, O, my Friends
That none of you shall be dead.

O, Duty! I shall run with thee
To the centre of the battlefield,
I promise to thee that we'll never yield
To the villains here you do see.

O, the enemies of our Nation!
Here do I stand -
Remember our country has sons
Who can die for their motherland.

O, ye Villains, let thyself see,
That the Fire has now broken free!
O, ye Fire, I doth permit thee,
To come and now engulf me.

With a last deep breath,
I looked up
At the shimmering Welkin:
The stars twinkling in the night.

It is always a Soldier's creed
To answer Duty's Call to fight.

II. Shooting Star

Twinkle, twinkle, little star,
The two great men entered their car.
Fate is playing the game of die,
The men let out a battle cry,
Mankind rages wars. But why?

The car rumbled through the plain,
The army all set to combat their bane,
The men of the military got down the car,
A tower was bombed and burned to char.

Fred and George met their allies,
In the barren land without green trees.
The sun shone above their head;
"Charge my men!" the General said -
The blood-stained field, a thousand dead.

Heavy firing in all directions 'nd heavy firing from both
the sides,
The Veil hides the horrors of war; the Veil hides
Their lives. A bang was heard behind the men,
The car just there, was now nowhere.

Fred, a hero, reloaded his sniper,

And shot the enemy like a viper.
George, his twin, was no less -
Fate is playing the game of chess.

Men fell, men lost, men died -
The Veil would hide this gruesome gore; the Veil would
hide
Their lives. But none paid heed, no one had the time -
The whole world's part of this gruesome rhyme.

The evening sun: the war knew no end,
They continued to die, with no one to tend,
The twins fought 'neath the night stars,
But then - a blast.

George then looked up in the sky :
Up, above the world so high,
"Twinkle, twinkle, little star.
 Freddie, you were just here but now you're so far, so far."

III. Call of Duty

As he stood adoring nature's love,
The Phoenix soared right from above,
The peaks around, all clad in white :
And Apollo shone behind, dazzlingly bright.

And carving the hill, into the plains,
The serene streams cross'd mountain chains :
And there he stood, right on his trek,
In front of him, an unfinished climb to check -

Down stood the valley among the spurs,
Which had witness'd death o'er those years -
The call of the clarion pierced the air :
Soldiers had known no rest, no care -

The guns thunder'd, and the man rush'd down -
Swift as a stream, the warrior gushed down,
Away from the summit: into the valley, among the spurs,
Which would witness death o'er more years.

His trek to the peak throbbed for his return,
He fired at the enemy, they were set to burn.
He was a warrior, a soldier true,
The Sun went down, the tawny sky turned eerie Persian

blue.

The night was silent and dark,
But who can forgotten that shot and spark?
It took his life and he lay dead,
The stream flowed into its mouth, the blood was shed :

The unsung shone as a star in the starless night -
For he answered Duty's Call to fight.

IV. Valorant

The sky glistened like coal in the dead of the night,
Like an eerie umbrella shrouding all light -
You wander for light, like a tramp;
But 'tis the Bold who requires yet not a lamp.

Danger determines to play hide and seek with thy Fate,
You feel exhausted and decide to wait,
But 'tis the Bold who mocks at the face of Hazard;
It is the right time for Danger to retard.

Trouble then turns out to be Danger's wildcard;
You are too late to realize that it has teamed up with
Hazard -
But 'tis the Bold who invites Strength, at his side,
The Bold does his duty, and Courage is his guide.

The night is still dark, but Hope brings a light,
To aid Strength and Courage in their virtuous fight;
You then decide that there is no point for you to wait,
Courage and Strength will save thy Fate.

V. Fatal Flaws

Too good to be good :
Thou art a slave of thy ego;
Thou is not perfect, thou has a drawback;
Man is but mortal - a needle in a haystack.

Too proud to be proud :
Thou art a slave of thy words;
If thou achieves a thing, thou says it aloud:
Man is yet another unit of the crowd.

Too confident to be confident :
Thou art a slave of thy false hope;
If thou does not toil, thou might as well fail;
Man is yet another character to the Tale.

Too ambitious to be ambitious :
Thou art a slave of thy dreams;
Caesar housed Ambition, who invited Death to Home;
Man is yet another Plebeian of Rome.

VI. The Detour To Darkness

Where the mind is full of fear
And the head is hung low-
The Earth compell'd to weep a tear,
For man today has chos'n to bow
Before the Deadly Sins -
What a shame!
Man is made an animal -
Their temperament is but the same.

Where knowledge is bound
And the world has been broken up
Into fragments by narrow chauvinist walls -
Where Nature wails and therefore she calls
"Balance yourself, O man!":
She thinks he can
For man, in the past, used to hold her dear
But today has he left for sure,
Mother Nature shivering in fear.

Where words have lost themselves
In the depths of lies-
O man, close your eyes and hear the cries
Of the civilization which staggers,
Being stabbed with daggers

Of mutual rift, rivalry, and enmity -
Human being has forgotten being human-
What a pity!

Where Sloth stretches his arms
Towards failure, bit by bit,
And the obscure steam of reason
Has long 'go lost its way,
Into the dreary desert sand of dead habit.

Where mankind has taken a detour,
To the road of eternal darkness,
To the necropolis of development,
To the Netherworld of ruthless crimes -
O, ye Supreme Creator!
Let my country awake in these times.

VII. Spring Will Always Come Again

The petals of the dawn bloom in the spring,
When the songbirds on the tree begin to sing -
With blossoms lively and lovely,
The tree is ready to bring
Joys to the whole wide world.

But the summer Sun scorches the bark
Of that tree with flowers, and we must mark
That the tree grows older and reaches middle age
But by looking at it, one cannot gauge
The burdens it is bearing.

And finally in the autumn season,
The flowers wither: there's a reason -
The tree is laden with the heavy wood
Of the responsibilities of adulthood.
So the tree becomes less lively.

And finally when winter comes,
We slowly cease to hear the hums
Of the birds. The old trees seem to be torn
For the leaves are shed and the flowers are gone.
The tree now grows older and older.

The life of the tree has now come full circle,
Is there any hope for joy to unfurl?
There is, for spring soon knocks again -
Again, there is a ray of light.
Again, the great old lively tree,
Is ready to grow and put up its fight.

VIII. Fireflies

We walked happily through the jovial field:
Prahlad had triumphed again, and Holika had to yield.
We were hailing the victorious who had always been
pure -
The evil would always meet such an end for sure.

The fire was ignited in the midst of the ground,
There was a buzzing amidst which I could still hear the
sound
Of fireflies chirping in the grasses tall,
I saw one, then two, till I could see all.

I was rejoicing with my parents and friendly faces,
Walking through the crowd of men carrying canes,
In the large crowd, there were no traces
Of enmity. The festival indeed makes friends from banes.

The satellite was at her zenith when we sighted-
The wood was lit and the sacred pyre ignited.
The fire was exalting to embrace the firmament:
It rose, it dazzled, it swayed, it bent.

The flames were dancing, and growing and swelling,
At the base of which burning embers were dwelling,

It was the defeat of Vijaya's cursed incarnation,
It was the victory marking the world's salvation.

Agni, who is the messenger to Heaven,
Rose further upwards; the sparks came out of their den -
Those sparks from the flames flew into the sky:
Fireflies winging in all directions, low and high.

The rising fireflies sang in joyful trills,
They're accompanied by the steam engulfing evils,
That had plagued mankind centuries ago,
And still plague our minds in a thousand forms or so.

The white steam was the steam of purity,
It calmly and violently spread through the entire city-
Peacefully purging the minds of men,
Granting warmth beyond space and eternity.

The steam banished the Devil out of sight,
And even his cruel allies were destroyed.
There were fireflies in the grasses shining their light.
And there were fireflies filling the welkin's black void.

The festival understands our feelings and lends
Moments to savour with family and friends.
I looked at my parents, and they smiled for they knew,
I had understood what the festival truly intends.

The glowing fireflies spread all throughout -
Leaving us smiling and completely spellbound.
No one knows how glad I had been when
There were fireflies in our hearts and all around.

IX. Walking by the Sea on A Dusky Evening

What waves these are I think I know,
They might not know who I am though:
Yet they would play with me: I would be stopping here,
And they would douse my feet and come and go.

With the fleeting waves washing my feet,
There did I stand by the spirited sea,
Watching the water flow back and fleet
And fill my heart up with glee.

And there I picked up some grains of sand,
Small pebbles and rocks- large gifts from waves,
Ah, yet I know that they themselves had
Borrowed it from the rivers carving their ways thro'
caves.

As tears of my joy fell into the sea,
Like the river falls down from the mountains great,
I let the playful waves hoard and be
The owner of what I had given them of late.

And then I walked along the shore,
Letting the water tickle myself:

Then it receded backwards more and more,
And I left my footprints on the coastal shelf.

I looked as far as my gaze would go,
Apollo was dipping further below
And gifting the welkin a veil of red
As she welcomed the sea to the nuptial bed.

I smiled and glanced at the frolicking sea,
Eagerly going 'way to meet his happy bride;
Knowing that the footprints I leave behind me
Would be evanescing at night with the rising tide.

I had come and I would go,
But the sea would frisk forever.
My footprints would be thus erased from sand:
Whom had time and tide waited for ever?

But still I was smiling, in the dimming light,
For I had always known, under these orange tints,
That I was walking over the erased footprints
Of someone who had walked here yesternight.

X. A Traffic Experience

This growing city is a wild beast:
It has never been quite quiet, at least.
In man and Nature's game of chess,
Has the urban city made any progress?
It expands and grows in forms and modes,
This growth has jammed its own wide roads:

There is always an ant-like rush: a ceaseless gush,
'midst which the vehicles suddenly begin to shush -
When the light in the corner goes amber, then red.
And then these insects suddenly stop dead.
The buses line and the cars now cram
And blow their horns in this traffic jam.

The honks, the blares,
The sighs, the glares
Spare neither men nor women,
Neither the young nor the old -
'tis the same story in the hot, the rain and the cold.
The hour-long minutes seem to bring them down,
During which they glance, they stare, they frown.

Transiently, the hustling metropolis
Is as silent as the necropolis:

But not for long as man knows not to wait,
And it appears as if he is always getting late.
So there is always some noise to disturb the equipoise,
But we must wait in the traffic for we have no other
choice.

The babies wail and the children cry,
But worse, the adults almost seem to die -
They grumble, they moan,
And complain and groan
Out of boredom which impairs their rest and care,
They are restless as if they are trapped somewhere.

Amidst this hustle and bustle of stationary noise,
There might be an air-conditioned car at poise.
Where a young adolescent at the age of fifteen
Might have been looking around and would thus have
seen
That he had had enough time to write
An entire poem in the unwavering red light.

He too would have cried,
He too would have wept a tear,
He too would have grown
Somewhat restless to hear
The blaring siren of an ambulance
Ringing somewhere in the distance:

No man can know the value of time,
Till each second becomes richer than gold.
As the boy continued to compose his pastime rhyme,
No man gave way to a man who was old.
The boy looked up and began to stare -
Midas had rendered all cars immobile in sight,
And the red siren continued to blare
In the now-foreboding, persistent red light.

XI. The Social Dilemma

Where the mind is contorted low,
And the phone is held high -
We scroll thro' posts of sort and kind,
Leaving our footprints all behind.

We spend hours on social media -
Post and chat and continue to scroll.
Are we really learning how to socialise,
Or just losing our reins of self-control?

Yet, social media is a platform
To express our thoughts and learn -
To keep up with the changing world
And direct our thoughts into a new bend and turn.

But seldom do we use it thus.
And hence, we oft do waste our time-
I do not criticize social media,
But ourselves, indeed, through this rhyme.

It is we who should use the media,
And not the media who should use us.
And the diplomatic solution to this dilemma
Is to place the situation thus:

A coin has two sides,
And so does life,
And so does every entity.
It is up to us if we
Want to float on this sea-
Or drown and immerse
In this online city.

XII. Aves

I weep silently, every moment,
Each second that passes by;
I miss the blue firmament -
That endless gleaming sky.

I miss them every moment, I do :
My spirit, into pieces, is sapp'd.
Mercy! O man - what is my fault?
Wherefore do I be trapp'd?
Within strong links of iron bonds,
Wherefore do I be trapp'd?

I remember, I remember,
The great trees, dark and high,
I used to sail across them swift
Into the endless sky.
Where are those flights -
The perpetual heights?
Wherefore do I be trapp'd?

The dense green forest,
The glittering East;
The treasure chest -
The birds and beasts

And butterflies and bees
And so much, in the lively trees :
I miss all of them -
Those were my elation,
Now replaced by partition and separation?
Mercy, O Man! Prithee, tell me
Wherefore do I be trapp'd?

My green wings to-day do long
To embrace that burning East,
My red beak to-day does cry
To kiss the Welkin, once 'tleast -
I miss the gurgling rivers and orchards
Where I was used to feast!
Mercy, O Man! Wilt thou now tell me -
Wherefore d'you trap this avian beast?

I want to weep more, but cannot cry;
No wish to live more, but cannot die.
Mercy, O Man! Tell me, O Man,
Wherefore do I be trapp'd -
Enslaved as a bondsman:
Still so trapp'd?

XIII. An Ode To Childhood

The echoes of history
Resonating each day in my ears:
The mirror of Erised
Reflecting those good, old years -

The echoes of the past
Pulling me back into good, old times :
The world of dreams,
The world of lullabies and rhymes.

The echoes of the clock - tick 'nd tock,
O cruel Time! Cannot thou pause thy tread?
Let me find a way out
Of the labyrinth of envious Hatred.

The echoes of Time
But now sound mild,
For I am aware that once again,
I can never be a child.

XIV. Cherry Blossoms

Calm was the Valley, and so was the Hill:
None made a single noise: all was perfectly too still -
The Valley was hiding among those spurring Uplands
Who would rise up to embrace the blue-eyed Sky with
both hands.

Fate woke up after slumber in bed;
Fate fluttered its third eye, and went on to tread;
Fate went to seek the Valley concealed.
(Those Hills with amulets would be this lowland's only
shield).

The Trees of the Blossom had gifted this earth,
With colours of Lotus: the pink petals of new birth -
And the Valley veiled itself, as shy as a bride,
She was running away from Fate to protect her blooming
pride.

The prophetic Welkin let out a cry,
Tears of sorrow seeped down from its eye,
He knew the near future, and the cruel game of Fate
Which is played by the whole world even to-date.

What Fate decides might not always be right -

Even Heaven and Hell knew that Nature was at fight
With herself, when Fate approached the Valley adorned
in cherry;
'nd wise Sun then knew that the sunset would be scary.

Midas froze the young boy lying behind the bush,
He could only hide when he saw the predator ambush
His own brother, who was shot in front of his eyes,
Banished to the black void beyond the black skies.

He could only see his brother's soul sublime:
Too young to know why he died before time,
Too young to analyze Fate's deceptive ploy:
The Firmament could only weep for the boy.

Truth is often lost in the pages of time,
Getting lost each second as I sing this rhyme.
Often, the one who tries to bring it out before the world -
Sees enmity, envy and macabre misery unfurl'd.

The prey had run from the predator for hours:
The boy and his brother had their feet lined with scars.
But he could, at present, only hide and stare:
As his brother left the unjust world, leaving him to
despair.

But then a loud shot, as silent as the dead,

Turned the flowers of the Cherry from pink to red.
Everything was silent, everything was still.
Calm was the Valley, and so was the Hill.

XV. Darwin's Racehorse: The Daruma's Creed

As I continued walking on the stony concrete
Which all felt so hard beneath my feet,
I looked at the flickering street lampposts,
And the errors of the day haunted me like ghosts.

I was treading to weary my own soles,
I was treading for my heavy eyes to see pale ghouls
Of the faults I had made during the day,
As I walked at night in utter dismay.

I looked towards the electric pole where there used to be
Some years ago, an old green tree,
And the wires now were an intricate maze
Like the branches of the tree at which I used to gaze.

I wished if only I could now return
To the far end of the street. Then, I would turn
Towards the playground where we used to meet,
Notwithstanding the cold, the rain, or the heat.

The breeze sweeping our faces as we used to swing
Towards the welkin and the cosmic ring
Of fire which gives energy to nature and earth,

And we swung towards the firmament's divine hearth.
But now am I too heavy to go up,
Too grounded to the material reality,
Left to lead a life full of errors and faults
Horses are forced to race, unlike young colts.

No swing would suit me,
But I could always slide,
I could strive to rise up,
Then automatically let myself glide
Or rather fall down, at once, towards the ground,
Destiny and Fate would bring me round,
To the same zero from where I did start:
(I could easily play the tragic hero's part.)

And I could also resort to the merry-go-round,
Which rotates around life's derby-ground.
That is what life has become, after all:
Rising and then falling because of a single wrong call.

I wish I could once again become a colt,
And gallop in the open fields at my own desire,
But Destiny now asks me to race and halt -
For I am a grown-up horse, who cannot choose to tire:
And each man struggles for existence in this race,
And we will have to, whether or not we admire -
We would all have to be a racing horse, and we all can

be,
Till Fate takes us to that burning pyre.

Thus, I could always start again when I fall,
Like the single tree in the distance which still stands tall.
The fittest survive in life, and I could be the one,
It is not necessary to be a horse - I could be a man and
run.
When error brings us down, we should not grimace;
For we can still stand up and continue to fight in this
race.

All attempts to succeed have been worthy praise -
Even after all this time? Yes, always.

XVI. The Hen That Lay The Golden Eggs

Seated at a distance, I was staring at the tide
On an afternoon of my trip to the countryside,
When the farmer's son with his glass of ale,
Sat down beside me and narrated his tale.

"You and I have heard a story old:
There was once a hen laying eggs of gold.
A farmer owned it; he slowly grew rich,
But one day, his palm began to itch.
He believed if he could kill the hen,
If he could stab it and then slit it open,
He would find in it a treasure chest
Of golden eggs, which would be the best.
But he lost his normal share in pursuit of more,
And they tell us every time when we hear this lore:
That greed is the biggest enemy of man:
Is it not bad to interfere in Destiny's plan?

"But yesterday I might have seen something strange,
The story has evidently altered, so let it change:
My Uncle had such a hen, without fail -
Who might be a kinsman of the one from the tale.
The whole town knew about that hen,

Which used to lay myriad eggs of gold,
Things are completely different though, this time then,
From what we had heard in the story old -

"The hen used to daily lay an egg of gold,
And every time it did so, it was told
Words of praise and given extra grain,
So it concocted a plan to have extra gain:
All its golden eggs on a single day
The avaricious hen then decided to lay:
To be praised more and fed more, more and more
And it emptied whatever it had in store.
It laid all its eggs just yesterday,
And my Uncle decided that 'twas okay
To collect all but still earn more somehow,
For he had a cunning plot in his mind now:
He became truly super rich,
His palm too then began to itch -
He knew that the hen was now of no use,
So he decided to trick the villagers into a ruse:
He summoned all the villagers and announced before
them
That he will sell the hen for the richest bid,
There was unrest in the village and total mayhem -
They were all tricked into my Uncle's stratagem.
The greedy hen then got sold.
Tho' no longer it can lay those eggs of gold:

I might pause and let you take hold
Of how much the world has altered the story old.

"The one with power in this material world,
Will see success e'en with his greed unfurled -
But the one who lies on the lower platform
Will surely pay for the same error in some form.
I know not about good and bad at all,
But I will let you hear my personal call:

"I have zero issue with a change in the tale,
For Uncle did buy me a glass of ale."

XVII. The Man With Two Faces

I was walking by the street at night,
With not a single soul in sight,
Wond'ring: would it be any different at day?
For man has surrendered his soul to foul play.

Walking thus in darkness by the dark street
I was thinking if in this world of deceit,
There is a single man who is true to himself -
Such men are extremely rare to meet.

Men wake up in the morn:
To see the polished mirror
Which has now become forlorn,
Out of utter horror -
For it fails to show the self
Of men who mask themselves,
Failure fills itself with terror:
O grave and piteous error!

The world is full of lies,
And pretentious ties,
Cats will begin to howl,
And wolves will sound their cries.

In the day, will hoot an owl
In the pine tree o'er there.
Fair is foul, and foul is fair:
Elephants kill, and tigers stare.
Deer will hunt, and lions will share.
Man will begin to stop to fight.
Roots will grow upwards in search of light.
Thieves will report their own theft,
Nature will be freed from industrial heft.

Something about all this did not sound right:
Instinctively, I began to take a left.

As I passed the corner round the way,
Something flickered brightly in the building old,
But I stopped not to see what there lay,
For men who were wise had always told:
"All that glitters is not gold.
Judging books by cover will bring but dismay."
So, I made up my mind to move forward,
But suddenly, I stopped dead in my way.
Suddenly, I was drawn to the flickering light,
Which suddenly began to glow stronger,
And I started running with all my might,
As the path suddenly seemed to grow longer.

There were voices in the air,

Silent whispers, evil laughter,
The men in town had told me not to dare
To walk on the roads after
Two in the night,
But I did not care.
I ran, and ran, towards the source of the light.
The deceptive moon began to glow brightly -
(The moon has no shine of its own).
Had I taken their word too lightly?
No, I was not afraid of walking alone.

As I neared the flickering light,
I stopped when I saw a horrid sight,
Which might have sent goosebumps down your spine:
But for me: I was completely fine -
The strong light was coming from darkness,
'nd it now began to glow dim.
There was a man with two faces,
He screamed; I just shook hands with him.

"Thou art true to thy nature,
And little evil stature.
Thou roam'st at the hour,
When evils are most free.
So listen what I would say, e'en to Ravana,
If he suddenly appears before me -

My friend, I have seen many men
With more faces than thee."

XVIII. Being Human?

What has happened to thee, O ye Human Being :
Ruthless you are, not less brutal!
How has thy gifted soul of gold,
Failed to discern what is vital?

Might thou be the lightest feather,
Carried away by the gust?
Or thou might be galvanized not :
An iron alone can simply rust.

Cannot thou say no to the blind Dhritarasthra,
And heartedly embrace Yuddhishtira's reign?
For if wise Sanjay fails to speak,
The entire Hastinapur suffers unbearable pain -

It is Kaliyuga, the reign of man,
But thou has never known how to rule;
Homo
sapiens sapiens might alone think,
But mankind is the wisest fool -

Human being has forgotten being human, no doubt :
What can thee do but sit idle :

'nd in one lone corner of this world
Lay untouched the Gita and the Bible.

43

XIX. The Grey Chessmen

Human beings are living chessmen
In the huge checkerboard of life -
They walk out of their little den
To conquer hardship and strife.

The infant in the ward
Is a pawn in its own accord -
His minute feet scurry across the street,
The white and black chessboard:
He takes a single step, or sometimes two,
On he knows not what road.
Often he stumbles, often he falls,
Sometimes his path is marked by brawls
For chess is not an easy game -
And Life herself hurdles the path to fame.

As a young chessman,
The innocent child plays
For the virtuous white side.
But he fails to fathom
When he starts to slide
Towards the dark black blaze -

But as he grows up,

He dwindles and swings
'tween the good and the bad wings -
So he is exposed to fault
Which forces him to come to a halt
In the roller coaster ride
That soars thro' Life's tide.

Yet Life supports man
In his time of need,
And thus supports an adolescent
To discern mankind's creed.

As an adult, he is capable
To handle capricious Life
And now is he stable
To overcome the strife
'tween the black and the white
Thus he decides 'tis right
To mix hope and dismay
Into an exciting shade of grey.

The pawn is now promoted
As it is now coated
With hues of quality and kind,
Adding layers to his labyrinthine mind:
The promoted pawn
Can now assume any form,

For Life compels one, now and then
To step out of the norm.

The grey chessman
Sometimes plays the sturdy rook -
A strong castle that can
Withstand the storm and brook.

The grey chessman
Sometimes plays the valiant knight -
A prudent, courageous horseman
Who puts up a brilliant fight.

The grey chessman
Sometimes plays the bishop wise -
He can discern what path to take,
For he knows what is virtue, and what is vice.

In the chessboard of Life
With chessmen giant and minute,
Man finds himself exposed to strife
And struggle and contest and constant dispute.

But he realises he is not alone
For his loved ones care for him -
And that inspires him to move forward
With others as a team.

When sixteen pieces are arranged
Together in two rows,
Standing united on one side,
They can boldly face their foes.

Therefore in this game of black and white,
Man finds himself fit, e'en as grey -
For life indeed is a recurring loop
Of hope combined with dismay.

And thus should the grey chessman
Focus solely on putting up his fight,
For even though Life sometimes seems unjust,
She always does what is right.

And as the grey chessman
Becomes so old that
His hair too becomes grey -
He finds the happy key of life,
And enjoys the light of the day:

When the grey chessman once realizes
A lot has Life truly lent -
He'd learn he has always been a King,
Each moment that he has spent.

XX. Ninety-Nine Point Eight

I thought I'd traversed the whole path,
But now, I see the last of lanes -
The roads they had said to take are taken -
But the one yet unravell'd still remains.
Hence, a road to be travelled still remains.

O, now I see the coast,
I do. I've already sailed the most,
I have, of the voyage 'cross the endless sea.
Tho' almost an inch, but still the shore
Stands far away from me.
I know there's yet a lot to see.
I know there's yet much more to see.

I have raced with spirit towards the finish line,
And I can see it run towards me.
Racing thro' the welkin, the land and brine,
Still, the trophy is yet not completely mine
Though it may appear to be.

The crowd have both jeered and cheered,
And I've answered them well - so fast have I steer'd.
The trophy screams my name -

O, I have heard.
I shall not rush but carefully propel forward.

I have prepared for years as the student of life,
Overcoming conflict and stress and strife,
Excelling time 'nd 'gain in the test of time,
Placing forth good verses in the worldly rhyme -
Yet, it all depends on the final leap:
To swim on the surface, or get the pearl, goin' deep?

It seemed I had written the whole poem of life,
But the uninked last stanza still remains.
I have traversed the whole path that was rife,
But still am left to tread on the untrod lanes:
The road yet to be raveled still remains.

XXI. Ninety-Nine Point Nine

The journey of a thousand miles
Began with a single step on yon road -
The journey brought with it a million smiles,
When million people joined me on-board.

The ship has almost reached the shore,
But I feel that there is still some more -
The voyage continues and the ship sails on,
It still sails in the sea through dusk and dawn.

What I had desired when I began to dream,
Comes unto me, and it doth seem
That a final boost will lead me to say
That I have successfully trod 'cross this way.

Each man is a pedestrian, and so am I,
Who walks freely 'neath the golden sky -
It shimmers in the light of the sun at morn,
And studded with gem-like stars when the moon is born.

No man is perfect and so the journey
Is never a hundred and never complete:
But still the pedestrian must approach his goal,

And fight in gale and storm and heat.

The pedestrian can never walk alone -
He needs those whom he can call his own:

To them, I have many a promises to keep,
And miles to go before I sleep -

The last few miles to my destination,
The last few to go before the night is deep,
Some more to go before the celebration,
Some more to go before I sleep.